We Decorate The

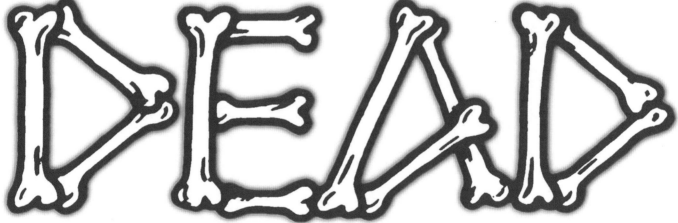

DEAD

A "Día de los Muertos" Celebration

"Las Flacas"

We Decorate The

DEAD

We decorate the dead!
That's what we do
We decorate the dead
'Cause someday we'll be dead too

We decorate the dead
So the dead don't die in vain
We decorate the dead
To alleviate the pain

We decorate the dead
'Cause the dead must live on
We decorate the dead
With poetry and song

We decorate the dead
And with each and every breath
We decorate the dead
Until we're laid to rest

"La Familia Lopez"

We decorate the dead
Prepare their favorite feast
We decorate the dead
So the dead may rest in peace

We decorate the dead
It should come as no surprise
We decorate the dead
Because it makes us feel alive!

We decorate the dead
Because life is a deadly dance
We decorate the dead
While we still have the chance

We decorate the dead
To celebrate life
We decorate the dead
To look death in the eye

"La Calaca"

Los Katrines

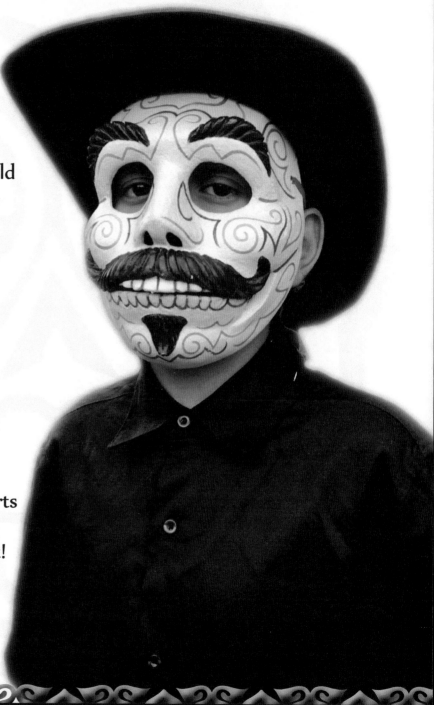

We decorate the dead
The dead both young and old
We decorate the dead
Because their stories must be told

We decorate the dead
'Cause it's our way of giving
We decorate the dead
To prepare the mortal living

We decorate the dead
For those who are dying
We decorate the dead
For those who are left crying

We decorate the dead
Because the dead live in our hearts
We decorate the dead
So that the dead may live as art!

Las Calacas - ready to perform. Unicamente en Arizona!

If I Die
TOMORROW

If I die tomorrow
I won't really be dead
My spirit will be free
To roam the earth again

Si me muero mañana
Llora un poquito
Mejor ponte a cantar
Algo bien bonito

If I die tomorrow
My life was good
I gave it all I had,
I did the best I could

"Dancing Calacas"

Si me muero mañana
por fin voy a volar
A pasear por el Cielo
y luego regresar

Please don't forget me
When you stop crying
If you remember me
Then I will still be alive!

Si me muero mañana,
que bendición!
Estaré siempre vivo,
en tu Corazón!

If I die tomorrow
Please don't be sad
Although life is hard
There's more good than bad

Si me muero mañana
Me haces un altar
Al estilo Mexicano
Hay que celebrar

If I die tomorrow
Tell everyone
Dead or alive
I'm having fun!

"Olliin Yoliztli Ballet Folklórico"

LA CALACA

In Ancient Mexico, before the coming
of the Europeans to the American
continent, there existed no word for
"death." Leaving this life was referred to
as "Mikiztli" and means "transformation."
There was no end to life but instead a
transition into another.

Mikiztli is represented as La Calaca
[Kah-LAH-kah], the smiling skull mask
of Mexican artistic tradition. La Calaca
has come to symbolize resistance and
affirmation of indigenous roots.
It is used extensively during the Mexican
holiday of Día de los Muertos—
"Mihcailhuitl"—to honor ancestors.

"Los Calaqueros"

The Calaca expresses acceptance of death because in Mexican culture when someone dies, his or her life is remembered and celebrated. Día de los Muertos falls on November 2nd, but in Arizona the celebrations begin as early as September and continue until early November.

The Calaca has become essential as an artistic icon and is a testament to the cultural renaissance that is today's Mikiztli celebration.

We Decorate the DEAD

"The Flight of Quetzalcoatl"

CULTURAL COALITION

The mission of Cultural Coalition, Inc. is to foster community engagement and provide unique cultural programs and processes dedicated to the promotion, education and development of Indo-Latino artists in Arizona.

Cultural Coalition, Inc. began as a grass roots organization of artists and community activists in the summer of 1996 to develop new and innovative ways to address important social issues while encouraging the participation of communities, schools and individuals to collaborate in the creation of neighborhood arts programs. We have produced annual cultural festivals, theatrical plays, and performances for libraries and educational institutions throughout the State of Arizona.

Our largest event is the Annual Día de los Muertos PHX Festival, which takes place in downtown Phoenix on the last Sunday of each October. It is free and open to the public. More information at: www.diadelosmuertosphx.com

The Día de los Muertos Celebrations in Arizona were started in 1980 by artist members of Xicanindio Artes, (now Xico) who are also the founders of Cultural Coalition, Inc.

ZARCO GUERRERO

Sculptor, mask maker, performance artist, Zarco has dedicated his artistic endeavors to create positive social change through the arts. The artist has exhibited his sculptures and masks in Mexico, Brazil, Japan and throughout the United States.

He is the founder of Xicanindio Artes, now Xico, Inc. and the Cultural Coalition in Phoenix. He has been instrumental in the development of Chicano Arts statewide.

Zarco is the Artist in Residence at ChildsplayAZ, and the creator of El Puente Festival funded by the Doris Duke Foundation.

Currently he is a Master Fellow with the Southwest Folklife Alliance in Tucson, Arizona.

CARMEN DE NOVAIS GUERRERO

A musician, arts educator and community activist, Carmen led the popular Latin band Zúm Zúm Zúm and still performs with the Guerrero Family musicians. As a visual artist she has done photography and now jewelry which she exhibits as part of the popular Latina Artists Collective The Phoenix Fridas.

As Executive Director of the Cultural Coalition she produces the annual Día de los Muertos festival and events, as well as theatrical plays dedicated to issues of cultural literacy and social justice.

DIADELOSMUERTOSPHX.COM

cultural coalition

Second Edition
Published by **Cultural Coalition, Inc.**
Cover picture: ELEVATE DanceWorks
Poems: "We Decorate the DEAD" and
"If I Die Tomorrow" by Zarco Guerrero
Artwork and Masks by Zarco Guerrero
Text by Carmen De Novais-Guerrero
Photographs by José Muňoz
Book design by Yolie Hernandez

ISBN-13: 978-0692546123
ISBN-10: 069254612X
Copyright © 2015 Zarco Guerrero and
Carmen De Novais-Guerrero
Printed in the United States of America

"La Ofrenda"